THE EMPTY BOAT

WINNER OF THE 2004 T. S. ELIOT PRIZE

The T. S. Eliot Prize for poetry is an annual award sponsored by Truman State University Press for the best unpublished book-length collection of poetry in English, in honor of T. S. Eliot's considerable intellectual and artistic legacy.

Judge for 2004: Diane Wakoski

The Empty Boat

Poems By
MICHAEL SOWDER

TRUMAN STATE UNIVERSITY PRESS
NEW ODYSSEY SERIES

© 2004 Michael Sowder
All rights reserved
Printed in the United States of America
New Odyssey Series
Published 2004 by Truman State University Press, Kirksville, Missouri 63501
tsup.truman.edu

Cover art: "Eight Views of Omi: Autumn Moon at Ishiyama" by Hiroshige
        courtesy of Gallery Sobi
Cover design: Shaun Hoffeditz
Body type: Minion
Printed by: Thomson-Shore, Dexter, Michigan

Michael Sowder is assistant professor of English at Utah State University. He lives with
his wife, Jennifer Sinor, and son, Aidan, in Cache Valley, Preston, Idaho.

Library of Congress Cataloging-in-Publication Data
The Empty Boat : poems / by Michael Sowder
  p. cm.
  ISBN 1-931112-44-4 (cloth : alk. paper) — ISBN 1-931112-45-2 (pbk.: alk. paper)
  1. Nature—Poetry. I. Title.
  PS3619.096E47 2004
  811'.6—dc22
                             2004009381

For Eileen Wall, Kathleen Sowder, and Jennifer Sinor

—three graces

and in memory of Walter T. Sowder

Contents

Acknowledgments

CutBank: "Cuervo Thoughts on the East Rim"
The Evansville Review: "At the Rehabilitation Center"
Green Mountains Review: "Ikkyu"
The GSU Review: "My Godfather's House" and "Cleaning the Face of the First American Bank"
Poem: "Watching Crows"
Poet Lore: "Lightning Whelk," "The Gulf," and "My Grandfather from Kentucky"
Southern Poetry Review: "Learning Names"
The South Carolina Review: "Watching Orion," "Fishing, His Birthday," and "The Lost Verse"
Sow's Ear Poetry Review: "Elegy for Ford"
Sundog: "Falling Asleep"

The manuscript's poems on crows were published together as *A Calendar of Crows* (Grand Rapids: New Michigan Press, 2001), winner of the 2001 New Michigan Press Award.

"Falling Asleep," "Ikkyu," "That Drink," and "May in the Kingdom of Hsuang Tsung" appear in the chapbook *Café Midnight* (with Margaret Aho) (Pocatello: Blue Scarab Press, 2003).

"Watching Crows" and "Crow With Lexus" appear in the anthology *Diagram* (Washington DC: Del Sol, 2003).

"Ikkyu" is forthcoming in the anthology *Beat the Black Wings: An Anthology of Crows.*

"Lighting Whelk" won the Bain-Swiggett Award in the Hopwood Contests at the University of Michigan.

"My Grandfather from Kentucky" was a finalist in the New Millennium Writing Awards.

"Elegy for Ford Swetnam" was a finalist in the *Sow's Ear Poetry Review* contest, the 2003 Dana Awards, and the New Millennium Writing Awards.

THE GLITTERING BODIES

*It is only as an aesthetic phenomenon that existence
and the world can be eternally justified.*

— Friedrich Nietzsche

LIGHTNING WHELK

—for Andrew Sofer

We went down to hear what the water said
where the tide was running out, leaving sheets
of water stained yellow, orange, and red
like notes from the clouds, clouds hung like a fleet
on fire. Pelicans sailed by, returning
with their carnival smiles—back to their nests
from day-long falling like darts in the churning
waves—now, with the sun's bright blood on their breasts.
A shell I pulled from the surf in my hands
rinsed to a lightning whelk—an orange-pink melt
swirled out to a blue-white crown, a sand-
cast comma of ocean thought—a heart dealt
to the land. And what dark, wrinkled hands spilled
this cup, that only a cry of the sea has filled?

Ludington Beach, Lake Michigan

The beach was a field of ice,
thick enough to walk on, though now
and again your foot broke through to sand.
We pulled our hoods around our eyes,
making tiny windows on the world.
Wind roared in over the surf, flattened
the down against our bodies, so my love
and I steadied each other as we walked.

Into the blind sun and minus-zero wind
you could look for only a moment,
but you wanted to look, for the wind
lifted the waves, and the sun
struck the risen water green
like cut glass that shattered on the shore
as if white were the essence of green.

Fish appeared beneath our feet,
thousands, identical—with silver sides,
sapphire bellies, and dark gray fins,
blue comets as far as you could see
frozen in every expression of fish life:
leaping, wriggling, squirming;
groups darting to one side,
others strangely arranged
in pinwheels, spirals, bracelets at our feet.

In the distance the lighthouse that marked
the trail to our cabin stood an hour away,
so we hiked upon the glittering bodies,

across a jeweled cemetery,
an illuminated manuscript
we were tongueless and terrified to read.

My Grandfather from Kentucky

was like a stranger coming into our house,
taking a bed at the end of his life.
And through his last months I sat with him—
making sandwiches between classes,
buying lighter fluid and Lucky Strikes,
changing his bed clothes, cleaning every day
his bedside toilet.
He talked about his old life—
the tobacco farm, cat fishing on summer nights,
his wife the best rifle shot in the county—
while the months became weeks, then days.

One morning in his room in St. Francis'—
where they moved him the day I found
his toilet full of blood—
he turned to me eyes as clear
as ten o'clock light, and asked
when I would take him across the street?
There outside the window cars stood gleaming
in the lot, where he said the grass was soft.

In the last days, there was little to be done.
He could no longer talk. Yet his eyes watched me
as I rubbed white lotion on his feet, and counted back
five generations until my father's family
disappeared in the Kentucky hills.

I wasn't there the last night.
I was out in the field behind the house.
The trees stood around the field like great dark birds
speckled with stars, and at a certain moment, *I knew,*

and kept walking—remembering trails with my father,
the first owl I ever saw, first indigo bunting
in its ecstasy of blue,
the first fawn, spotted and awkward,
all the exquisite strangers of the world
my grandfather released with open hands.

My Godfather's House

—for Jim Mersmann

Coming home to my godfather's house,
the big yellow house on the hill
where now he lives alone, I unlatch
and swing open the gate, and the dogs
come running—big dogs he raised for guarding,
but too much like him for that,
they won't stop jumping,
taking your hand in their soft mouths.

The yard slopes up under hickories,
hackberry, oaks, pecans. White doves
he raised and trained to stay
coo their five-note phrases. I come around front
and he's there on the porch, standing square
and smiling, blond hair and beard,
this man born on Christmas day.
We embrace like old friends and soon
are talking about the real things, naturally,
as though people talked that way all the time.

The house is full of silence:
a church he made a home
of secrets, little doorways, alcoves,
odd-shaped rooms, attic dormers
looking down on the distant city.

In an upstairs room that I call mine,
I sit at a desk by the window—a captain
in his cabin, and look down on the garden
we fenced together, posts we set,

orchard in newest leaves,
maple stumps around a fire ring
where we cook and drink late into the night
while koi hold steady under the fountain.

At night in my bed I can hear the water talking.

There over the hill leans the elm we trimmed
to let light into the garden. I perched
on a ladder as he pointed, and cut
branches that fell around him softly
like feathers stolen from the nest of some great bird.

These last fifteen years, I've seen him
maybe once or twice a year.
But what does that matter?
In those days we read Rilke, Neruda, Whitman,
and he showed me the names of things.

KILLING A CROW

I was twelve. I was angry.
It was the kind of August day when your shirt sticks
to your back, your crotch rubs sore,
and fights break out among boys like storms.
I went down to the basement and got my gun from the cabinet,
opened a tube of copper-colored BBs, filled my hand
with them, each notched and shining, guided them
into the chamber, put the tube in my pocket,
soldiers in a box, and went back out
into that heat—wasps and locusts buzzing.

I stalked down steps, past three terraces,
down a trail into the towering pines.
I shattered bottles, knocked over cans,
picked off soldiers as they struggled up hills.
But there wasn't shit to do.
I sat under a loblolly and lit a Lucky Strike
stolen from Dad's ashtray, hot and bitter.

Then I heard it, high overhead—
caw! caw! —mocking me.

I flicked the butt and picked up the gun.
Aimed and waited, till
no cawing, no wind.
Click.

It came down like a weight
to thud on the ground
and lie in a heap

without a twitch—
a hole through one eye
slowly filling with red.
Goddamn, what a shot! Wait till I tell the guys!

I picked it up by the tip of a wing
and it opened in a black arc
from the ground to my chest,
a great black fan, like the sweep
of an arm embracing a landscape.

Holding it away from my body,
a little dazed, I carried it
up the trail, up the steps, back home.
I stood at the door for a moment,
then dropped it in the trash can under the stairs.

That night it came back
out of the sky
in a dream
like a falcon and seized
my outstretched wrist and held it.

At the Rehabilitation Center

We called him Ahab, the crow
with the missing foot, who lived
with his cell mate in hog-wire
between snowy owls
and turkey vultures.

On early mornings
when fog lay over the marsh
my love and I gathered stars
of cat food spilled outside the cage
and held them up to the wire

because crows are familial, their murders
are families. Parents make two- and three-year-olds
stay home and help raise the simps,
breaking up early courtships.
So, being familial, Ahab leapt up

to the big white limb in the cage
and took the hardtack out of our hands.
He'd leap back down to the floor,
wings unfurled, and stride on foot
and stump to his dish where he dropped
the snack in the water.
Then he waited, one eye cocked
toward the softening red star,
dipped his beak, threw back his head,
and swallowed with a shuddering of wings.

We did this again and again.
Sometimes the birds were fed cereal
and one day alphabet cereal.
And that day we put words in his mouth:
bug, fish, nevermore.

Before long he knew us by sight,
and we came welcomed
by whistles, clucks, and caws
we were beginning to understand.

Learning Names

All my life I heard him call her *Mother.*
Dad, can we camp out in the backyard?
Ask mother. Or, *Mother, can you*
pick up the shirts at the cleaners?

Now retired, they've left the city,
moved to a house overlooking a valley
in North Carolina. She tends tiny junipers,
rain trees, elms. He nails and glues maple and birch
for birdhouses, toys, and hand-carved signs.
In town on Tuesday and Thursday
they teach farmers, mill workers,
to read and write.
But they, too, are learning names:
evening grosbeak,
honey locust, yellow trillium.

In the quiet before dawn,
I sit under a lamp by the window.
A visitor now. I hear them stirring
in the next room, talking in low voices.
Outside the window, slate-colored juncos
are chirping and flitting in rhododendron leaves,
and I hear him softly say,
Kathleen, the way he must
have said it thirty years ago.

WATCHING CROWS

At dawn they're in the pines outside the tent,
cawing, anxious for the breaking
of camp. And when I hike out, they come
down yelling, landing with wings unfurled
behind them, walking around stiff-kneed
and haughty, lords of the forgotten and discarded.

I spooked one last night
out of a creek bed at twilight.
It came right at me, pounding
the drums of the air, flying
off through pillars of hemlock and poplar,
screaming its wild hoarse cry.

They say one appeared
at my great aunt's open window
and, drawn to what glitters,
flew off with her wedding ring
and a twist of foil.

From a cliff on Blood Mountain,
I watch one beneath me, oaring
the air over waves of hills,
shouldering its way to the highway,
to a gathering at some body
headlights froze in the dark.

At the sentinel's cry they will rise
in a cloud of wings

like pieces of a withered tree
breaking apart, floating upward.

They're always flying off,
peripheral, seeking the tangents,
never nesting at bridges, ledges, eaves.
My father one day walked out
the back door, drove nails
into a post and put clothes on a cross
he set up against their intransigence—
to tame his own wildness, I guess.

I think of the sky in their bones—
the way a crow never soars, but moves below, black,
across the valley green, like the shadow of a cloud
or a lost kite, a blind spot moving through the landscape,
a tear in the drapes, a fleck of night
shot straight through the summer day.

Reading Sylvia's Journals

Feeling like a thief or voyeur
peering in a window, a beachcomber after a wreck
picking up a blue bottle half-full of perfume—
I sit in the rare book room and open them gingerly,
like brittle manuscripts, pieces of Sappho,
feeling slightly drunk, giddy—the way I felt one night
in Charleston, South Carolina, with a woman
I would marry, our first night of sex,
walking down a narrow street, stars
big as dogwood blossoms. In a garden, I opened
a window, and we stole into the Catholic church,
and walked down the aisle in the colored light of stained
glass lit by a single street light, breathing the acrid
redolence of incense, votives flickering,
down to the altar, where I recited Latin
learned as an altar boy and we pressed
our lips at the place of sacrifice
in the thrill of mortal sin.

First loves, jealousies, rages, secrets
of craft. I read about her first meeting
with Hughes at a cocktail party
at Cambridge, when he took her into a back room and
      kissed her,
and she bit his cheek, drawing blood at first light.
I turn the pages as everything unfolds
in that long foreshadowing, as in any good Greek play,
but mostly I come for the words,
that wild incandescence
that keeps me up at night.

In dreams I see her out past the last blazes,
fled from the house of Atreus,
laying out her tents, high above the sea,
building signal fires, watching the East,
standing at the brink, pale
clouds clutching the moon,
knowing the shortness of time,
feeding words to the fire, sending out pigeons,
falcons, the black world racing under her feet.

WAPITI

Late October. Grizzly country.
My wife and I sleeping under stars.
I wake to perfume of alpine fir
and a shadow coming toward us.
A great bull elk
grazes the meadow above,
pawing at the ground. Clouds of breath
hover around his face, and when he lifts his head
the sky is filled with antlers, like hooks
thrown for stars. *Wapiti,*
we are lost, this woman and I,
we are losing each other in the world.

Wind tosses the tops of cedars. A glitter
of stars and runaway clouds.
The undertow of sleep pulls and pulls,
washing the world away.
A clatter of hooves along the edges
of dream comfort like sounds in a kitchen
heard in childhood beds, saying,
Sleep, child, no danger is near.
Tonight, you are safe on open ground.

CUERVO THOUGHTS ON THE EAST RIM

—for Jon Hershey

In starlight the pink granite seems lit from within.
We sit on a ledge thrust over a canyon
as if on the prow of a ship.
Up the trail behind us
yellow windows flicker through pines.

We left plates on the table,
bread crusts and salmon bones,
whiskey glasses by the fireplace,
and a cowboy whining on the radio
'bout how he'd rather be in a pine box
on a slow train back to Georgia.

Draco slinks over the horizon.
Red and green lights
skate through western stars.
Orion releases a satellite.

No moon, you say, and flick on the flashlight.
Its silver scope dredges the darkness
but pulls nothing up. It can't reach
the far cliffs, or the trees waving
their arms in the dark hundreds of feet below.

You knock my knee
with the *Cuervo.* I drink
and in my chest, a white
crow opens its wings. I say:
You know, I think we've used every failure
to cover up the one before.

You spit.
Take another drink, set the crow
on the rock, stand up and say:
Don't fall off the goddamn cliff.

As your footsteps fade I lie back
in a crevice in the rock,
and wrapping my coat around me settle
in warmth beneath the wind.

Colonel Joshua Lawrence Chamberlain,
professor of rhetoric lay down in a field of snow
and blood not far from here, the night between
battles at Fredericksburg, lay down between two
dead men and pulled the coat of one over his face
to keep out the snow and the moans of the dying
and then slept through the night.

Tugged by the ropes of sleep,
I'm drunk on my watch, lying
in this crevice, like Queequeg in his coffin,
covered in hieroglyphics, the *Pequod* plunging
through oceans of night, under southern stars,
the great, luminous emptiness saturating, holding all things.

Tattoo

1.

At first it feels like your skin tearing,
a meticulous burn, a wasp sting.
Breathe into it, he says, and I try to stay present
to the inky needle hammering away like
a hummingbird behind my shoulder.
I stare at the purple floor. I look up
where Brando, Marilyn, Elvira gaze down
with the compassion of saints.
Doing okay? he asks, lifting the needle,
wiping my skin with a cool, alcohol-dipped cloth.
Not too bad.
I'm putting in the blue highlights, now.
He starts again, and I drift off…

2.

A morning fishing with Dad.
We set the canoe in the fog-covered water.
He held it with both hands as I got in
and then he turned and said, *Mike, look!*
Above the canoe, a dead crow hung upside
down, a foot tied to a branch,
wings open as if frozen
in a headlong plunge to earth.
I cut the string, knew I would keep it,
and carried it up to the cab of his truck.

In the afternoon, we went in through the doors
of *Ocoee Taxidermy,* a still-life wilderness

where rattlers coiled with fangs exposed,
rainbows leapt through the air,
a wildebeest pawed the ground, grizzlies lunged
with claws spread wide, gazelles, ibis, lions stared,
while a pack of coyotes howled in a corner.
It's like time has stopped, Dad said.
Nothing dies, like trying to keep
it all from vanishing away.

A boy at the counter handed us brochures
about safaris in the Congo, fly-fishing the Snake,
swordfishing Costa Rica. On the wall we saw photos
of a mustached man and a dark-haired woman
kneeling over a gazelle.
Colonel's 'round back, he said.
We went in through swinging doors
to an inner chamber, a wide, bloodless
charnel house, work tables
spread with hides, heads, claws,
hammers, vises, tweezers, everything
reeking of formaldehyde and glue.
Three helpers in aprons leaned
over some feathery work.

The *Colonel* walked up smiling, his eyes
like blue mica. He took up my crow
in his hands like a preacher taking up snakes,
put his face right into the down,
and inhaled like it was the first day of spring.
No odor at all, he winked. *Wings in good shape.*
How do you want him? I'd say head forward and down,
beak open, cawing. He knew something about crows.
170 dollars. Be ready in seven months.

3.

Now I look over my shoulder
at my blue and black companion,
a trickster appearing only in mirrors
who lives inside the skin and out,
a token that won't get lost, something
for keeps, like a promise
or a scar, a mark of the clan,
a cross in the road from which you never go back.

DRIVING TO NORTH CAROLINA

ten days after Dad's death, Highway 24
surrendering itself to spring.
I keep replaying the moment
I heard the word
as the sun broke
rose over Appalachian ridges
and thought: *Well—the battle's over,*
the one I fought with him my whole life.

Tomorrow I'll wade the Nantahala,
wearing his boots, throwing his flies
three miles into the forest
where two cascades tumble
opposite ridges to the river,
and there, under the mists,
find the rainbows.

I hurtle across Kentucky,
count red-tailed hawks
in the highway trees.
Lime-green sprays fountain
over hillsides, orange fire
drips down banks, dark cedars
gilt-edged, last year's beech leaves
still holding on. Farm fields washed lavender:
henbit: *Lamium amplexicaule:*
Greek, for thread—Latin, for clasping,
embracing, holding on.

And I start to understand
the elegiac turn, the heart's sense
of the fallen risen in translucencies
of spring, a presence like a rainbow,
a few feet away, holding in water under the falls.

THE GULF

Fields blurred away into a blank
August sky, radio stations infected
with static. Hot air beating at the windows
couldn't take the sweat out of my shirt
though I'd been breaking speed limits for 300 miles,
crossing into Georgia, down 27 into dusk.

At the Shell station outside Cave Spring
I pulled open the busted screen door,
and a woman in a white Mustang
with a sandaled foot pointing
at the bloody sun smiled
and didn't look away.
Dark blond hair like yours.
And when I came back out
into the rosy-fingered light, locusts
chirring, fireflies beginning to blink,
she smiled once more, holding back her hair
while someone I couldn't see drove her
away down the two-lane.

I stood in the perfume of honeysuckle
and gasoline, feeling slightly sick,
like someone in a David Lynch movie,
as the scene of the night before fluttered
again before me: Cook's Inlet,
outside New Orleans, your pier
under a string of yellow bulbs,
air conditioner busted, the house aching for a breeze.
The neighbor's radio turned up for Aretha.

I was looking at the curtains, edged
in yellow light, thinking how they'd
never stir, never lift with a breeze, like a hand
held out to us, to anyone that night.

And we lay still, the talking over.
You softly sleeping, my toe
touching your ankle,
and the Gulf lapping beneath us.

Rose Bush

In the morning, white-tail prints
covered the ground.
I went out to the cliff
where the bark of a pine
curled red before a cloudless sky.

But I want to tell about the wild
rose bush that day, a fountain of branches
thrown from the ground high over
my head, stems lined with green campfires,
a great wave of green bells.

I remembered something about you then.

And as I turned to leave
delicate thorns for a moment
held my ankles and let go.

In the Dentist's Office, Reading an Old Issue of *Poetry*

Some things are better off dead
till the body's resurrection.
Root canals aren't meant to save lives.
Crowns serve appearances.
And I've had it all before. The novocaine,
the twelve little apostles—
threaded needles, each thicker, longer, to get
down to root tip and take the nerve out.

So here in the waiting room, leafing
through last April's issue of *Poetry*,
torn and smudged from lying
under the seat of my car with tools, cassettes,
and crumpled Coke cans, who'd have thought
I'd find between these pages a single strand of hair—
too long, too light, too fine to be mine.

Last April. We walked the levee
of the Oostanaula. Bluets, dandelions
spread like constellations at our feet.
Swallows turned their purple backs
and skimmed the surface of the river.

I was a lawyer then. Now I scan lines.
On the left page, someone admits a *desire to be done*.
On the right, a couple of regular Bonnie-and-Clyde
lovers, right out of the movies, cornered and going down,
but sticking together to the end—
filling the night sky full of holes.

But endings don't always turn out that well.
And now the blond assistant is calling my name.
Sometimes we take them lying down—
one, two, three, four, five killings
just like that.

CROW WITH LEXUS

A crow hops in circles
beside the neighbor's SUV.
He stares at the reflection in the door,
which offers little more than fescue,
daffodils, a house with pines, and a cloud-strewn sky.
With wings like a cape, he swirls
around and drunk on his vision
plunges into the door.
Stunned on the drive, the little devotee
collects himself and begins again
his ritual dance. But the approach is atavistic,
naïve in our self-referenced world,
our finishes transcending all his codes.

Once goldfinch, orioles, painted buntings,
far out of their zones, fifty or more
lay dead across the pavement of Peachtree Street,
in colors so rich and strange they seemed
blown out of some shattered paradise.
The meteorologist said: *They fly into*
the skyscrapers that reflect the sky.

We've all heard it:
a knock on the window
a fall to the ground
saying
The sky is falling,
The sky is falling.

ELEGY FOR FORD

—for Susan Swetnam

that wisdom comes alone through suffering
—Aeschylus

1. April 2001

The flyways were full of glittering strings
of ibis, onyx necklaces flung hurriedly
across the skies, lines of text unhooking

from the page, unreadable auguries.
The marsh teemed with pelicans, coots, and kites,
stilts, wrens, hawks, grebes, yellow-headed blackbirds,

red-winged blackbirds clamoring for new life.
Cranes opened their great gray sails, and males bowed
and leapt in air, wagging their heads in wild

swaggering courtships. But this wasn't home.
This was a watering hole. Like them, see,
I too was heading north, north and down, down

to the Arco Desert—the Big Empty—
where the Little Lost River comes pouring
down to disappear in a dry, sand sea.

Around nine o'clock I was still crossing
the Bonneville, a desiccated fossil
ocean, when in my mirror a coyote

streaked across the highway, its fur ruffled
in my tailwinds. I knew then I was crossing
a line, some tide of this invisible

sea had turned, and everything was going
to change. I met him at the desert's edge
and we kept north, across the reservation,

running his pickup, that rust-eaten Chevy,
the land falling before us, the day mute,
shrouded in cloud. Sharp pyramid wedges

of rock loomed: Big Southern, Middle, Northern Butte.
We could see it was going to snow. Bearing
west, we saw INEEL, the site, come into view:

Idaho National Engineering
and Environmental Laboratory
INEEL. *(I kneel in the desert, sand running*

through my hands.) White hallucinatory
towers, walls and globes, pale like cancer.
The snow falling in a forbidding story.

At Craters of the Moon, we stopped and camped
where everything was black, black—the earth
scorched, and I walked with him (once a dancer)

leading me through lava, a land whose birth
was recent, still unfinished: slag crumbling
everywhere, talus, detritus, scoria,

Devil's Garden, Dragon's Head, weird shapes rising,
junipers burned up, their roots exploded.
And as we crested one hill, snow flying
like ash, he told me he was dying.

He walked on, breathing hard. An early vireo
calling out. And I looked at the black world.
I'd given him the *Purgatorio;*

and this like some *Inferno*, lifeless, sterile.
And as he showed me things he knew, I
felt, *No, pity is wrong*, even in this harrowing,

for he, the older, better poet and guide
was leading me and I saw him like Virgil,
and I knew he was teaching me how to die.

᭡ ᭡ ᭡

Morning. We climbed to a favorite, fragile
hanging valley, in the Pa'semmeroi,
past Larkspur Creek, Blue-jay Canyon, Saddle

Pass, above the Big Empty and the clouds,
where the sun lay yellow on willow bark
on a rill and a moose chewing new sprouts.

As for us, we had BBQ in Arco,
population 1,000, where an old
black couple from Walla Walla

brought steaming ribs, corn bread, collard greens,
potatoes, and sweet tea—all you could drink,
in this the middle of whitest Idaho.

And sitting with him, whom I'd only known
a year, who'd shown me many things, savoring
southern fare, I thought of an afternoon

when I stood in the sun on the corner
of Bourbon and Toulouse, outside the Absinthe
bar, a spring afternoon without one worry,

carrying through the streets of New Orleans
a book of Verlaine that a woman
I'd just met bought for me that morning.

Her name was Sulamith Chernoff,
and I stood on that sunshine corner
feeling as lucky as the day I was born.

2. September 2001

In a clear photo on *The Times* website, morning light
drenches the Brooklyn Bridge like a Tai Chi dancer
in a gold robe leaping from Manhattan to Brooklyn,
throwing cables of copper light
across the brackish North Atlantic
waters. The violet sky dotted with gulls.

To the right, in the distance,
the Trade Towers are exploding, black-orange
corollas of fire, those familiar malignancies,
blooming from their broken bodies,
with smoke that will blot the sun,
where photos will show
the people leaping from windows.

Later, Ford would tell me that the night
of September 10, before any of this seemed thinkable,
hours before it happened, he dreamed
he was falling in a burning elevator.

I take down from my shelf
the very best book I own,
and hold Walt Whitman in my hands,
joyous seer, chanter of songs,
uniter of here and hereafter,
wound-dresser, poet of America.

Tell me again, Walt Whitman, the one about
the Brooklyn Ferry, your eyes the color of the sky,
your head, everyone's head, haloed in spokes of light in the water,
tell me again the words thick with the love of strangers,
for the women and men leaning against the rail.

And I take down Hart Crane,
and read about the Brooklyn Bridge, harp
and altar, silver-paced, lifted into the arms
of the night, yet stage from which the Bedlamite
leaps, his red shirt ballooning as he falls.

And I go and get the film I love the most,
to see Nathan and Stingo and Sophie
drunk on the Bridge, drunk on whiskey
and Whitman and Crane and blind desperate love,
climbing the cables, shouting words into the night
that flash and disappear like gulls through
headlights, and see Sophie, carrying the secret in her eyes,
in her flesh and womb and at the corners of her mouth,
the world's dark secret, a wisdom too dark to tell,
that only music, and madness, and dying can heal.

3. February 2002

I kick a feathered body in the dark by the road—
white like the hoar-frosted sage,
spotted—a barn owl—some wreck of an angel,
its message irretrievable.

The invisible sun backlights the eastern mountains,
casts red on a western falling moon,
stitches alpenglow brocade upon the edges of the world.

I finish my ritual pee on Red Rock Pass,
study the valley below, that vanished sea,
now a pool of darkness, a few ranch lights
coming on. I step over
the owl and into my truck,
head down into the shadows,
a mile of so ahead of the light.

Inside the instrument-panel-lit pickup, Krishna Das
leads all the singers in a chant to the great mother:
Jaya jagatambe, he maa, he maa durgaa
maa kaalee durge—namo namah.
Making the mountains stranger, bluer, icier.

I'm on my way to his mountain fastness, where
he lies dying, following his cancer like Virgil
to where none of us has been,
but Persephone, Odysseus, Aeneas, Christ.

The sun lights the world,
and I count the deer on the road
released by melting snow, so many

botched sacrifices by priests
with sin on our hands. *Great Mother,*

make me a heart of glass,
obsidian hard as an Aztec blade, so that I do not turn
away from the death of a friend,
but sit there in silence, if need be, quiet
as an owl. Let us watch the red moon sail,
clearing the scoria, this broken ground.

4. April 2002

It seemed he didn't go until all the arrangements
were made—the marshes full and greening,
the flyways crowded with honking,
the very bodies of the finches

turning to gold, when everywhere
in fields still patchy with snow,
calves and colts were falling to the ground,
wingless and surprised, the secret
of the earth in their startled eyes.

5. August 2002

In our hands, the ashes look different from
what any of us had imagined, blues and greens
in the whites and grays and bits of bone.

I stand by his wife, Susan, and by my Jennifer,
up on the Big Southern, above the Big Empty,
some redneck kids on the far edge of the cliff

laughing and shooting clay pigeons two thousand feet
above the desert. Through luck and grace I'm one
of twenty-four carrying ceramic vials

of him, like Osiris to all his favorite mountains.
Susan sings, "I'll Fly Away," and for this
Wordsworthian, I say, "My Heart Leaps Up,"

and for this dancer, say, "The Windhover,"
and then it's, *so long, Ford,* and we toss him out,
into the Big Empty. We drop some tears

and walk back, while those kids we cursed,
those pranksters he would have nodded to,
keep laughing like cranes and shooting off their guns
like it was all some kind of wild celebration.

Fishing, His Birthday

With adams, caddis, tricos, light cahills,
blue-wing olives, royal coachmen, chartreuse trudes,
green drakes, blue duns, black gnats, Nancy's quills,
Joe's hoppers, yellow humpies, purple chutes,
prince nymphs, pheasant tails, Eileen's hare's ears,
telicos, flashbacks, Jennifer's muddlers,
Frank bugs, sow bugs, zug bugs, autumn splendors,
woolly worms, black buggers, Kay's gold zuddlers,
clippers, tippet, floatant, spools of leader,
tin shot, lead shot, hemostats, needle nose,
rod, reel, vest, net, boots, cap, shades and waders,
gortex shell and one bent Macanudo—
I wade in a swirl of May-colored water,
cast a fine gray quill, the last tie of my father.

THE EMPTY BOAT

*The way back forgotten, hidden
Away, I become like you,
An empty boat, floating, drifting.*

"Written on the Wall at Chang's Hermitage"
—Tu Fu

WATCHING ORION

I'm lying on the hood of my Honda Accord,
my face cold, the car warm beneath me,
a quiet knocking in the cooling engine,
my front wheels halfway in the lake.
I'm watching Orion drag his sword across the south.

There was too much wine at the dinner party,
so I drove out here with my head
full of spirits this Indian summer night—
at this cold, uncertain season when bullfrogs croak
in the dying reeds, and fish leap in the darkness.

In the trunk on a paper bag lies a crow
I found frozen outside Angell Hall,
one of the thousands that in winter turn
elms into waves cresting black.
Tomorrow I'll come here again, balancing
a hangover like a head full of nails.
In a homespun ritual, I'll take feathers
from its wings and bury it, or leave it out on the hill
like monks leave brethren on Tibetan cliffs—
the flesh to be picked from their bones, and the bones
gathered up, ground into dust, mixed with millet and butter,
and set out again for the airy raptors.

                  Castor and Pollux
are chasing the heels of the hunter, and you,
my love, born under their sign, now far away,
out of reach, streak canvases with the violent colors
of childhood. For three years, divorce has been eating at
the edges of all our things, memory and dreams.

But eventually one day you wake up, and feel your legs,
and think, *I'm walking*—and start looking
around, see rocks, hickories, slate-colored juncos,
orange lights around highway trucks,
ordinary people at the neighborhood market.

Now a fish jumps at my wheels where they wait
halfway in the water, and I watch Orion
turning into himself—clothed in lights,
dissolving into stars,
while Corvus, naked and glittering,
climbs the eastern sky.

Three Days in Grand Island

—for Keith and Joline Sinor

When peacocks open ocelate fans
and guineas coo over eggs in the straw,
a cat prowls the yard, llamas,
Saber and Josie, aloof as priests,
peer down from a grassy hill,
where trees bow with apricots,
cherries and plums by a garden growing
more flowers than food, you know
that, on this emigrant's Platte River Road,
midpoint in a free fall, a whole life
left behind, and showing up on a summer night,
in a towering, careening, filthy, Ryder truck,
three cats in the cab, one crapping and crying
for 600 miles, the kitten exploring pedals,
scratching at semis through windows
as they hurtle by through the rain,
you know you've come to a good place.

Woken by clover and the sound of bees
and meadowlarks, I carry coffee
to the garden where Joline kneels in the dirt
wearing a smile she learned from flowers,
and walk down to the pond where Keith
and Jennifer stand at the forge
bending fire-pink rods of iron,
Saber and Josie condescending from above.
On a bench swing we sail above the pond,
that cup of sky, crisscrossing
time's pendulums and talk of
the coming of cranes.

On the third day, we raft the Platte,
discovering too late the depths of the drought,
the river lying above the plain.
Traders ran aground fifty times a day,
dragged boats across the sand,
oxen yanking wagons and kill-mules killing mules.
Sunburned, heat struck, hours from nowhere,
we pass a cottonwood and a moment
when play turns to care, and we drag
each other in the raft, down miles of sand,
seeking ribbons of water for another ride.

Long after midnight, fed and refreshed,
I lie down by my love, and slipping into sleep
in prairie moon silence, dream of Li Po,
half-frozen on snowy paths,
reaching a candlelit mountain fastness,
taken in, where boys and girls serve
millet and mushrooms,
hot tea and chrysanthemum wine.
The old woman plays her *chin*,
and talk winds late and wistful.
Then he lies on a mattress, soft beyond reckoning,
there under the window
where the dragon bangs at the shutters
harmless the whole night long.

At the Edge of a Field

Wind plays in the silver poplars
shimmering with light.
A cold moon culls the ground
for shadows.

I stand at
the edge of a field.
The fragrance of fallen apples
hovers around my ankles.

I hear the waters of Cranberry Creek
down in the woods,
whispering to each other in the dark.

Are they also nervously waiting?
Someone is coming
who walks like mist on the river.

Waking Up

After a night of rain
coconut palms
clatter in the trades.

Mynah and dove call loudly out—
claiming their place
in the new arrangements of day.

A single white jasmine
flower—sutra
of the morning.

Former Attorney Offers Prayer
of Thanksgiving for His New Job

—for Ford Swetnam

I thank you, God, for this poem today, whether or not it'll be
    any good,
and for a new home in a town called Preston with a desk under
    a window of sky and the cries of cranes,
for a full moon that rises over the Bear Mountains at twilight
    and falls past mountains at dawn,
for a river named Bear that tumbles out of a canyon, meanders
    by our house, with hot springs, kingfishers, osprey, and
    trout,
for our neighbor, Ezekiel, who comes to the door with
    cucumbers and carrots for the forgiveness of sins and
    hopes for our redemption,
for new words, like *jack-Mormon*—reminding that even in
    Zion apostates like dandelions grow,
and *gravity water* which runs down hills, which the city doesn't
    charge for, which rises over fields in silver jets, swords
    crossed against the desert sun,
for my commute across the bed of an ancient sea that one day,
    14,000 years ago, broke its dam and spilled north for
    hundreds of miles,
for the oranges and reds of autumn spilling down watersheds
    of Oxford, Bonneville, and Scout,
and aspens that etch the fir-dark peaks in gold,
for light dawning clear as the Mediterranean,
while magpies rise from the nameless dead of the road where
    they dine in tuxedos—Republican cousins of the crows,
and for my arrival in Pocatello, where treeless hills fold over
    each other with a Renaissance love of the naked body,

a U.P. town of rails, cowboys, and poets who, it has been said,
    actually—and I shit you not—like each other,
and for a boss who says, *Write poems, not briefs.*

For this is a beginning, and it's good to be beginning,
as Whitman and Merton and St. John of the Cross said,
for we'll always be beginners any day we're alive.

And now the streams are tumbling with syllables,
and the sea's rhythms are printed on the land,
cranes trace calligraphs across the evening sky,
and rocks break like words on the ground.

May in the Kingdom
of Hsuang Tsung

Li Po, knight errant, walked into
a country wine shop,
took off his sword and embroidered cloak,
and asked for a bottle of local wine.

A young man sat at a table sipping
the same dark vintage, writing.
Li Po noticed his well-formed characters.
The young man continued without looking up,
gazing out the window from time to time,
where sunlight caught the falling blossoms
and a breeze carried in the perfume.

Miffed at the rebuff, Li Po sat down,
took out his brush and paper
and began grinding ink.

Before long both were very drunk.

Then Tu Fu looked up. Outside a hawk cried
where gibbons screamed.

The two went out and practiced their swords.
After many flashes, Li Po had won.
They bowed. A little crowd dispersed.

Inside the tavern they gathered up their things,
exchanged verses and ordered another bottle.
Hand in hand they went down to the riverbank
to wait on the dock for the coming of the moon.

Down the Etowah

—for Virginia Carstarphen

I watch your strong shoulders and arms
dip and draw the paddle,
bring it forward spilling an arc of falling
silver in a rhythm steady from practice.
Poetry came from rowing.
Sunlight gleams on your hair
lying in braids on your shoulders.
The water parts as we go,
and leaves behind a V like a flock of geese.

On the shore, green yellow poplars
flutter like giant chimes.
And willows lean over the river
laden with dew and new June leaves.

We round a bend and the bank falls away
towards the Cherokee ruins,
green pyramids gazing down as we float by.

The river is almost still, glassy,
a carpet of leaves and sky where kingfishers
dive and we glide through.

And if we paddled the sky
as the river pretends, we'd dip
our blades in wonder
no deeper than now.

FALLEN CROW

At dawn I drove over black wings,
thought for a moment then turned around
and eased back down to the curve where they lay.
I pulled over and cut the engine.
The road lay in the silence
of fading night, the sun just lighting
the high green wicks of pine.
Nobody in sight.

I got out and walked over to it.
Its head, round as a black plum,
lay cocked to one side, as if puzzled.
The right wing broke at the shoulder.
I picked it up and thought of nestling it in leaves
in the woods but knowing what my Cherokee
friends would do, I laid it on newspaper
in the trunk and took it home.

Behind the house I knelt on grass
wet from melting frost and unwrapped
the bundle of glinting feathers.
The blackness drank every color
spilling over my hands.
Soft down covered its head and breast.
Talons hard and strangely large
hung from its body.
Eyes, acorn brown.

I imagined aloud the roost
it must have flown early from,
flight loosed from a bow.

I praised the life of a fallen crow
and with shameless hands
pulled feathers from its left, unbroken wing.

A Lesson

It's hard to get right—
the way the sun
flower of joy
blooms out past
the reach of desire,

whorls of green, soughing
of branches, afternoon light
open

when the stomach
is empty
and you've sat a long time alone.

Joy is rooted in emptiness

in not running away
from your own pain.

It's hard to get right.

Like right now: behind the black branches
the West blooms red.

I go into the cabin
and pour my first drink of the evening.

CHRIST'S KITE

—for Ted Haddin

Our horses picked their dark way
down a rock trail towards Cuzco—
the Incas' sacred city.
Scared my mare might stumble yet
tired of being scared, I closed
my eyes, surrendered to her
animal way of knowing.
I looked up then and I saw
the Southern Cross for the first
time. A diamond of stars
without a center, more like
a kite, I thought, than a cross.

As the saddle's gentle cradling
rocked me nearly to sleep. I
closed my eyes and half dreamed I
saw Him sitting cross-legged
in a field bright with daisies.
There was a flock of children,
grown-ups, old people. He was
smiling a big smile, unroll-
ing a piece of papyrus
(which Pliny the Younger called
more supple than fine linen),
or perhaps it was raw silk
from China, I couldn't tell,
or maybe a miracle,
I don't know. He formed a cross
out of two slender cedar

branches and attached a tail
of rags. He tied a string on—
hemp twine unwound from a stick.

Jesus, he was laughing! All
of them were laughing, leaning
back, some showed their broken teeth.
Women looked at him, and he
didn't always look away.

He finished his creation,
got up, and I swear to God,
he took off running! I mean,
Jesus, running—through the fields
with boys and girls, fishermen,
priests, soldiers, tax collectors,
dogs yippety-yipping and
people yacketty-yacking,
children screaming wild with joy.
He raised his hand and the kite
swept up—wagging its crazy
head! Everyone's eyes went up.
They called it a miracle.
Everyone wanted to hold
the string that joined the heavens
to earth. And when everyone
had stood for a moment like
the anchor of heaven, he
cut the string and it sailed up
into the blue. A voice said:

Behold my beloved son,
with whom I'm well pleased. I am

that I am, I mean, I was
angry, hungry for vengeance.
That's done now. Just look at how
that kid makes everyone
happy.

And Jesus smiled to
cut that cord, knowing all the
nightmares of Gethsemene,
Judas, *Pieta* had fled.

And they all lifted their heads
to see the kite that Christ set
like a jewel in the sky.
And then to their amazement,
it drifted slightly south.

IKKYU

Drifting, I lean
back in the bottom of the boat—
rocked in starry water.
Bullfrogs thrum and groan.
Black pines ring
the shore making lashes
for a starry eye, while everywhere
insouciant, scattered fireflies push
light out of their bodies.
A peel of moon crowns the lion.
The dragon is slain by a star.

One summer night, five hundred years ago,
a solitary monk drifted on Lake Biwa. Suddenly
(he later said), many years of fitful sleep,
a life of fear and anger fell away
on hearing the midnight cry of a crow—
as the world dissolved into luminous nets of light.

After that, they called him *Ikkyu*—
One Pause—for the gap between life and death.
He called himself *Crazy Cloud,* drifting
here and there.
But what he did just then
was go back to his village,
to his people, to the brothel and sweet bed of Lady Mori.

THE STRANGENESS OF CROWS

Winter begins like this:
A cold, clear twilight,
black branches crack-
ing a pewter sky.
Songbirds not flown
south are all bedded down.
And me walking home
through empty streets.

Suddenly over the hills,
over the trees and roofs,
mounting the freezing air,
legions of crows come flying—
hundreds and hundreds
in wild, bat-like flight,
black stars falling
filling the bowl of the sky,
yet silently—
not one crying out.

I sit down on a lawn to watch.

Seizing the tops of trees,
like leaves snagged on limbs in a river,
they sit in the gunmetal sky
hooded and robed
like Caesars over Rome.

And then, as quickly, they're gone.

I walk home dizzied
by the strangeness of crows,
that they are the way they are,
and the world the way it is
rather than otherwise,
that there should be anything at all
and not nothing.

In the Luminous Dark

—for Jennifer

On a balmy summer twilight—
our first dinner together—
we are eating flowers.

Love-in-idleness,
midsummer night's
dream of purple, scarlet,
creamy yellow petals
with wine.

Your head in my lap,
you say, *I am very drunk.*
Are you going to take advantage of me?

In the luminous dark of your bedroom,
we wrestle, and you lead my hands
to the brocade flowers
of your slip, along your long-stemmed
bones, to the chrysanthemums
and dark iris of your body,
your green eyes glistening with desire.

November Suns

Jennifer and I look down
on Swan Lake, Highway 91.
Next to us a young maple is curling
its dark orange leaves.

The sky falls asleep under a tattered quilt
of clouds. Blue holes let down lights
that telescope the land, flash on a farmhouse window,
the windshield of a truck,
turning ponds to silver, Cherry Creek to gold.

A shaft climbs toward us
arriving in a soft flood
and broken by leaves
prints granite
in patterns of rose.

Behind the tangled black trees
a dark orange circle slowly falls.

Only November suns
go down like this.

Things darken.
Clouds pull apart like batting.
Venus shines like a bead of mercury
spilled from the cup of the moon.

We break some sticks and start a fire.
For three days we will not go home.

Cleaning the Face
of the First American Bank

Pushing off from the skyscraper
into free air, without harness, swinging
on a wooden seat, his checkered shirt flying
from his waist, a bucket trailing from his seat,
clutching a twenty-story thread
he polished the glassy precipice
that said at ground zero:
Insurance For Your Dreams.
He moved like a marionette
or a spider riding a breeze.

My man!—somebody yelled—
and he's busting moves,
clapping, miming, moon-walking on air—
kicking his heals, shedding Newton's laws
like scales from his body.

And when I let my eyes go soft
the whole tower of glass, that ruled
the town like Rushmore, vanished
in a mosaic of white and blue
where two window washers clearing
each other's image swung together
in an empty sky.

Such faith he had in what held him—
not like a sinner hung by an angry string—
something else let him down
in that excess of April light
where he worked along the edges,
rinsing the panes of the sky.

Saint Francis in Ecstasy

—after the painting by Giovanni Bellini

—for Mike Carson

Called, he's come out from his cave
and stands outside himself,
barefoot in robes the color of wooden
tools and sandals dropped behind, arms
held out, palms up, sun-struck eyes.
A single elm reaches into gold.

Rock of pale turquoise, pale blue,
nearly white, is moving beneath his feet,
swirling up into cliff, a wave
leaping from the frame.

Beyond the edge of cliff, on the crest
of an olive hill, the red-tiled roofs
of a villa. In the valley a castle
with parapets, turrets, green flags flying.
This is the world.

In the foreground a shepherd stands
by his flock.
Very close, a donkey is watching—
looking across the chasm where

Francis is burning, rapt
in his robe
like a wick in flame,
lighting this portal, this passage
for our translation.

That Drink

More and more things
    kindle inside,
        incandesce.

More and more edges
    soften, thin,
        until all the transoms open

and you see how things
    are sunk and set in light.
        Then the heart

finds its mate
    everywhere.
        There are streams

where we are going.
    When the water bottle
        goes in the water

it always comes out full.
    I tell you, pretty soon, that which is inside
        and that which is outside

are going to have that drink
    they penciled in
        a million years ago.

May Morning, Snake River

The current slows and I lay down
my paddle, lie down in my boat,
and drift. Green stars line
maple limbs, pieces of jade
in lapis. Two eaglets pirouette
and light, flapping new wings.

A breeze stirs the bees
humming in wild riverbank roses,
filling the air with incense.
The easy current rocks me to
and fro, and I feel like a child
in his mother's arms. I catch

my breath when I remember
how the Han saw the Yangtse River
flow to the east then up
into the Milky Way,
down again in the west—
and I see my empty boat
filled with morning light
riding the sky-blue waves.

RIFLE RIVER

—for Jennifer

From our yellow wood canoe
we dip our black paddles,
cut cold, blue water
under an April sun, gliding
through flat, late afternoon fields,
toward green and violet woods.

We lay our paddles down,
as we always do, and lean back
closing our eyes to the brazen
sun, and let the boat find its
way, this way and that, a yellow leaf
its edges curled around us,
suspending us high over brook
and rainbow trout.

In a half-dream light I see
nothing, feeling your body,
its long, magic bones,
smelling sun in your hair,
hearing the flow and ebb
of your breath and the redwings sing.

We turn around and around as prow and stern
bump logs and the reedy shore
around and around,
a compass needle loosed from north,
spinning across the flat gold fields
toward the twilight woods lit
with redbud and laurel,
like lanterns hung out for a carnival
or wedding celebration.

New Snow, Ann Arbor

The Huron tumbles gray and blue
through the Arboretum woods. At dawn,
the snow glowed rose,
held blue in the shadows.
At eight it was blue and gold,
and at ten it was white and blue.
I looked to the south,
and the white became silver,
a field of lights, prisms,
like infinitesimal stained glass.
A cardinal emptied its quiver of songs
and as all the windows opened,
I could hear Eckhart reading a page
from his own book
how *the eye with which I see God,*
and the eye with which God sees me
are the same eye.

I stood staring, snowflakes swirling
through sun, landing on me,
melting into my coat
like arrows loosed
from a thousand invisible bows.

THE LOST VERSE

In your birthday-present aquarium
Hypostomus plecostomus
rests in the lap of the Buddha—
his body divided bow and stern,
half black, half pale tangerine,
like a yin-yang cigar,
or a half-lit submarine.

An algae eater, all morning
he's been sucking the scum
from the Buddha's body,
cleaning that great roundness,
hands and face, chest and thighs,
while Gautama sits quietly,
two feet under,
without
breathing.

All about them shimmer
the spangled host: neon tetras,
silver angels, prayer-flag Gouramis,
rainbows, fire mouths, pearlfish,
a water filter their only choir.

And all the while, there at the center
Mister Plecostomus lies
content, knowing how lost verse said:
Blessed is the scum of the earth
for it shall adorn the body of God.

My Friend Takes My Dog for a Hike

I see them crossing the southern,
meadowy slope of a mountain, fields shot
through with sunflowers, asters, clematis.
It's mid-morning—mid-summer. Apollo
wheels through the blue.

Krishna flushes a clutch of grouse,
runs circles and figure eights
in the blissful abandon of puppies.

They come to a spring where pebbles
glitter like seashells, and Krishna plunges
in up to her belly, bites the water
and drinks, looking up at Ford
with her one blue eye.

Leaping lightly from rock to rock
using his big gnarled stick, Ford thinks
his busted knee's feeling better
than it has in a long time.
He stops on the other bank, leans on
his stick, and takes a look around.
White-flecked, the indigo sea stretches
toward Africa. *Damn fine country*, he says.
Come on, pup.

At the edge of a cliff they sit
under pines in clover and thistle.
Ford unfolds cakes from a cloth
left at his door that morning

with a note calling them *ambrosia.*
Krishna gets some, too.
He drinks the sweet water, and Krishna
drinks from his wooden bowl. He leans
back with sun in his beard,
breathing the fragrance of sage.
Krishna digs in the dirt, lies down and closes her eyes.

They've got time.
They're not trying to get anywhere.
These are the days that will last forever.
My friend and my dog hiking the hills of Elysium.

Falling Asleep

—for Jennifer

You are sleeping
    when I hear them—
        hoofsteps knocking

loose rock,
    scraping the ground.
        Mountain goats coming

into camp,
    floating
        in moonlight on

delicate ankles,
    a ragtag band
        of angels.

I hear teeth
    tearing tundra
        in the dark.

The old couple on the trail said they
    found the lost boy—
        frostbitten, but alive.

Deer, he said, lay down
    beside him all night
        in the flying snow.

The last coals break and fall in
    muffled exhalations.
        The goats gone down

the meadow. Coyote yipping on the pass
    where a Milky Way arcs
        out of sight.

I nestle in my bag
    to the sound of your breathing,
        rising and falling

like the mountains around us.
    I float into sleep
        at ten thousand feet,

the night giving wings to our bones.

Afterword

الذيك صاحَ	vrana	烏	go-ga
vrána	*kraai*	vare—	كلاغ
corneille	*Krahe*	*corax*	alala
קרקור	varju	Mahkoto	Chro
corvo	鴉	*corvu*	bburung
gagak	*gogi*	krake	*cráwe*
wrona	corvo	ворона	*cuervo*
kumguru	ka ka	karga	kau wa

Notes on Poems

"Elegy for Ford": Ford Swetnam, poet, climber, and teacher at Idaho State University in Pocatello, Idaho, was the author of *Ghostholders Know, 301, Another Tough Hop*, and *Offer the Cup to a Friend*. Originally from Virginia, Ford came west in the seventies to climb mountains and became a mentor and friend to countless students, fellow poets, and writers. He passed away in April 2002. His wife, Susan Swetnam, author of *Home Mountains*, teaches at Idaho State University and writes in Pocatello.

"Watching Orion": Corvus— a small constellation adjoining Virgo in the south.